# Job Hunting

*The Perfect Answers to the Most Important Interview Questions*

# Table of Contents:

# About The Author

Hello,

my name is Sean Dematrés. First of all, I want to thank you for investing in this book and therefore in your future. I wrote this book because I never had a great education and therefore I was struggling many years to find a job that I actually liked. I was always stuck with work I did not want to do, if I had work at all. If you have a similar problem you came to the right place. This book teaches you how to become highly employable so you can choose where you want to work.

The reason why I wrote this book is that I noticed how much your job influences your life quality. Most of us work at least 6-8 hours a day and if you don't enjoy what you are doing even to the slightest, you are wasting your valuable lifetime.

I know that some of you wake up every morning, hardly being able to get out of bed because you already cringe just by thinking about going to your current job. And once you are there, you are constantly looking at the clock to see how much time is left until you are finally "free" to go home. This is a life nobody wants to have but a lot of us are stuck with. I know what that feels like, my life used to be just like that.

All the way up until my late 20s I just couldn't seem to get the jobs that I actually wanted. I was stuck with work I did not want to do and this feeling of not accomplishing anything in my dead end jobs was killing me from the inside.

When I was 28 I reached ground zero. I was alone, unemployed and broke. But I made my mind up and noticed I only had two choices. Either I will be stuck with jobs that make me unhappy and drain my energy for the rest of my life, or I have to change something about myself.

I had to make myself a highly employable person. And you will have to do the same.

This book is teaching you how can become a highly employable person by teaching you how to stand out at job interviews.

I had countless job interviews and I noticed that there are questions that are asked almost in every single time.

I can't give you the perfect answers, because every interview is different. But I can tell you what the intentions are behind these questions, so you will know exactly what to say and what you should rather keep for yourself.

By leaving a good and lasting impression at your job interviews, you will greatly increase the chances to be considered for higher paid jobs and positions that you actually want to work in.

Sounds good? Alright let's get started!

# Introduction to the Interview World

Everyone struggles with interviews at one time or another. You are probably here to help yourself overcome this issue. You are in the right place and already in the right direction! Hiring managers are looking for people like you that see they have a weakness, and find ways to overcome their struggles.

Included in the chapters below are tips, tricks, and advice to help you through an interview. You will learn the most common interview questions asked, why they are asked and how to answer them in the strongest way possible. There will be questions about you including: What are your greatest strengths and weaknesses? Where do you see yourself in five years? What are your professional achievements?

There will also be questions that you should prepare for about the company. Be sure to do your research beforehand as you will be asked questions such as: What do you know about the company? Why do you want this job? Why should we hire you? Be sure to be prepared for any questions thrown in your direction.

After you are through with this book, you will be an interview expert. Also included in this book is information about interview preparation, what you should bring with you to an interview, and best ways to be ready on the big day. Follow the steps below for your best shot at landing your dream job.

# Different Types of Interviews

With modern technology, companies are no longer limited to only face to face interviews. Before, a future employee would need to have a one on one, a panel, or a group interview. With new technology such as computers, phones and tablets, companies are able to give interview through telephone and video calls. This type of development gives so much opportunity to those who may live in a different area or have no access to transportation and also gives the ability to employee those that could be overseas!

Having access to different types of interviews means that an individual should be prepared for any type of meeting that comes their way. Have the material, knowledge, and ability to tackle any interview at any given time. Below is a condensed list of the interviews you may encounter during your job search. By having the knowledge ahead of time, this may give you the head start you need to be the right candidate for the job!

## A. One-to-One Interview

Usually a formal event, this is one of the classic interview tactics used. By using face to face interaction, a hiring manager is able to process your answers, knowledge, and body language in one sitting. It is important to be aware of all three. Also, one should be prepared to be interviewed by different people at different times. It is vital that an interviewee is always on their toes as they do not know who is watching their every move.

## B. Panel Interview

This type of interview is similar to the one on one. During this process, be prepared to have two to three people asking you questions. These employees will most likely be from different parts of the company, accessing your answers to figure if you are a right fit for the job and if you will be able to fit in with their culture. It is important to read their body language and mimic if possible. By doing so, it will create a natural flow to the relationship. People relate most to those who are similar to them.

## C. Group Interview

A group interview can be one of the more challenging of interviews. By placing people together, there is an immediate challenge. In a group setting, one person will be asking questions to multiple people. It is important to keep a settled nerve and be able to stand out of a crowd in a positive manner. Finding the balance of intelligent, knowledgeable, while being respectful of others is important here.

## D. Telephone Interview

The telephone interview is normally given before a one on one interview. This method can be used to get to know the candidate, catching them off guard. However, if you are applying to jobs and receive a call from an unknown number, always be expecting the call and be up to date on the company's information. By using phone calls, hiring managers can eliminate candidates based on their first impression. If one is successful at the phone interview, they are normally invited to a one on one interview in person.

## E. Video Interview

A video interview is one of the more modern ways to present an interview. There has been an increase of popularity for interviews through programs such as Facetime and Skype. By using modern technology, companies have the ability to select from a wider range of candidates. No longer are the business' constricted by location. Video grants the ability to perform interviews anywhere a person has the access to internet. Same as a phone interview, video interviews are normally used as a preliminary screening process. By having access to a video interview, it can show future employers that you are familiar with modern technology.

F. **Assessment Centers**

In these Centers, future employees are presented with certain tasks. These can include role-play, group exercise, presentations as well as written tests. The tasks can last between one and three days and are usually either done alone or with several other candidates. By having access to these centers, companies have the ability to not only asses the individual on their set of knowledge and skills, but also see if the individual can work well with others and fit in to the culture of the company.

# Before the Interview: How to Prepare

Whether you are an interview expert, or new to the work force, it is important to brush up on preparing for an interview. If a person shows up to an interview, dressed casual, hair a mess, stuttering over their answers to important questions: that is a sure way to not get the job. An interview is an essential time to make a stellar first impression. It is vital for a person to take the time and effort to prepare for an interview because more times than not, winging it will cause utter failure. If you are serious about landing your dream job, follow the steps below before even thinking about the interview questions you will be asked.

### A. Dress to Impress

Have you heard the expression: Look Good, Feel Good? Words could not ring truer in the situation of an interview. As stated before, first impressions are essential to landing a great interview. First thing, you will want to be aware of what the current employees are wearing. Are they extremely formal or formal casual? As a standard, you will want to keep your look basic and conservative. By doing so, you will give off a professional vibe but will not stick out in a negative manner. It is essential that your outfit is tailored, clean, and pressed.

While focusing on the outfit, it is also important that one keeps up with their personal hygiene. If you are aware of an interview coming up, it is suggested that you get a haircut, trim facial hair and also be aware of your nail health. These are all key efforts that a hiring manager is trained to look for. Be ahead of the curve and put your best foot forward in your very best suit.

### B. Know your Audience

This is vital. There is nothing worse than going into an interview without knowing anything about the company. If they begin asking questions and you have no clue what the business does, this is a sure way to set yourself up failure. Do yourself a favor and research the company as soon as you apply for the job. You should be familiar with their goals. What is the big picture of the company? In preparation, research of current news should also be done. By knowing more about the company, it will show true attention to the business. It possible, be aware of who is interviewing you. By getting names first hand, it will come across that you care more about interpersonal relationships. By having a name, you will have the ability to research the person interviewing you, granting you access to their background and reputation in the company. This knowledge may also be able to give you a head start in the interview process. There is nothing quite like making a person feel memorable and important, even if a majority of the interview is spent talking about your own set of skills. Remember, you are not the only person in the room.

## C. Resume & Reference List

Your resume and reference list are two items you will always want to be up to date. It is important that you have at least five copies of your resume with you during an interview. This way, you will be able to anticipate the hiring manager not having one, or a situation where there is more than one person interviewing you. By being prepared, this will give a good impression of your preparedness and organizational skills.

When it comes to your reference list, first thing: make sure that your references have all been contacted and know that you are interviewing for another job. You do not want to stumble across issues with your reference if they are unaware that you are either leaving the job, or are looking for a new job. By not contacting past employers, you may risk burning bridges. Make sure that your reference list has the following: name, title, organization and email address.

## D. Mock Interviews

Nothing can prepare you more than putting yourself through the interview before hand. Ask your friends to ask you the common interview questions. These questions and answers can be found later in this book for your reference. However, if you do your own research on common questions asked in an interview, it is important that you do not write down your answer completely. It is suggested that you write down bullet points, making your answer easier to recall during the actual interview.

During your mock interview, make sure you pay attention to everything from your answers to your body language. Be aware if you are fidgeting or using too many hand gestures. An issue many interviewees make is crossing their arms and legs during an interview. Try to avoid this at all cost, crossed limbs can give off a defensive vibe. Instead, focus on being calm and collected. Be aware of your posture and stance at all times. One can practice certain movements during conversation that can successfully assist getting the point across.

## E. Sleep

Despite an interview being high stress, it is to the upmost importance that you get your sleep before the big day. Use the week before to make sure you are prepped for the interview. Have your questions answered, your research of the company finished, and have your outfit picked out beforehand. The night before an interview, take the time to relax and not think of the process to come. Instead, focus on yourself and go to bed early. It is very important to get a full night's rest so that you will be awake and alert to the next day. Being at 100% is essential for a successful interview. Do not let your nerves cause your own demise.

# Interview Questions Involving the Self

During an interview, you will be asked a series of questions. These questions can range from questions about yourself, the company, and sometimes even random questions that seemingly have nothing to do with you or the job at hand. As a future employee, it is important you know why these questions are being asked, the type of answer an employee is looking for, and how to answer the question in an honest and beneficial way. Below are the common questions asked in which are related to you as a person. They can range from question about past experience, your skills, as well as your hopes and dreams. Be prepared for anything a hiring manager may throw your way.

## 1. Tell me about yourself

There is a high chance that this will be one of the first questions a hiring manager will ask. Of course, you will be prepared for this question because you did your homework! It is ridiculous to think that such a seemingly simple question can make people sweat so much. Here are the essentials you need to know while answering this question.

First, this question is not an invitation to recite your whole life story. The question is asked for the hiring manager to detect how you feel about yourself. The best answer will include reasons you at the right one for the job by focusing on your skills and experience that is most relevant to the job position. However, do not make the mistake of listing off what is already on your resume. The interviewer will most likely already have the resume in front of them.

It is suggested to use the Present-Past-Future formula to answer the broad question in the most tactful way possible. This means you start out by discussing what you are doing currently, then gracefully connect your past experiences with your present skills and how they built you to the person you are, and finish strong by discussing why you are excited for future opportunities with the company.

A very important piece to this question is to be true to yourself. This is a perfect opportunity to show the hiring manager your personality. If possible, try to stay relaxed during the questions. Though the interviewer is watching carefully and listening for answers that will resonate with them, by being relaxed, you will be able to think more clearly and give the best answer possible. After all, nobody knows you better than yourself.

## 2. <u>What are your greatest strengths?</u>

With this question, you will want to be true to yourself. A hiring manager is asking to see if you will be beneficial to the company. There are some people that have great professional strengths that would be better in other industries. Remember, the interviewer has a set of skills they are looking for in an employee. By doing your research beforehand, you will be able to judge if your strengths are fit for the job. If you decide to fib the answer to something the manager wants to hear, you will not be doing yourself any justice. A good interviewer will be able to see through the façade quickly.

An important factor of giving a good answer to this question is by being relevant to the job position. Target your skills to support why you would be top choice for the position. For example, if it is a job that requires customer support, instead of simply stating that you have good people skills, you will want to address yourself as a persuasive communicator. By selecting your vocabulary carefully, your language can set you apart from other people applying for the job.

While listing off your strengths, do not forget to provide examples. Be sure that these situations were in a professional setting. Your interviewer will want to see that you have the ability to take control of a situation, work well with others as well, and be able to tackle any situations sent your way.

# 3. <u>What is your greatest weakness?</u>

It can be understood why many people feel this question is either a trick or a trap. The truth is, the question is used in order for the hiring manager too gage your self-awareness as well as your honesty. There are a few ways of getting around this question but the biggest tip that can be given is to always keep it positive. Now the question is, How?

It is suggested that during your interview, you should focus on a struggle that you had in your past. By describing the issue, you can spin it into a positive situation by stating that you are aware of the struggle but are working to resolve it. For example, if you are a person who has struggled with public speaking, discuss ways you worked to improve. Give examples such as: volunteering to speak during meetings, or practicing speaking in public with friends. The person hiring you is looking to see if you are honest with yourself about being an imperfect person, and accessing how you handle a negative situation. They will be searching for a person who does not quit when faced with a challenge. It is important to be an individual who seeks to always improve.

The number one thing you will want avoid while answering this question is to say nothing. If you say nothing as an answer, your hiring manager will have checked you off the list at that very moment. By saying nothing, you give off an arrogant vibe, which is an attribute employers do not want in their environment. Stating you are a perfectionist is another answer that should be avoided. The hiring manager will be able to see right through you. If you avoid these answers and remain honest, it should be smooth sailing onto the next question.

## 4. Do you have any professional achievements?

Now is your time to shine! A track record of achievements is always impressive to companies. They are looking for employees who take action and make a difference at their job. Make sure you take advantage of this opportunity to set yourself above the other applicants. In order to give the best answer, it is suggested to use the S.T.A.R method which is made of four steps. By following the steps, an interviewee will be able to give the most thorough answer possible, sure to impress the hiring manager.

The first step to take is to set up the Situation. Give the important details of the situation by providing context. Where was the situation and when was it? You'll want to choose a time that you are truly proud of, preferably one that is more recent. True, all achievements can be impressive but your employer will want to know that you are constantly making great achievements and making changes at your job.

The second step is to describe the Task you were required to complete. With this, you will want to describe the challenge presented to you and the expectations held during the situation. Be sure to go into detail about what needed to be done and why? The hiring manager will be curious as to why the situation was so vital at the moment.

Third, describe the Actions you took to resolve the situation. Be sure to elaborate on what actions you took, how you changed the situation, and if needed, tell the employer what tools you used to benefit you. By doing this, you can show off any skills you have. For example, if you are handy with computers and it was necessary in the situation, show it off!

Lastly, you will want to finish strong by explaining the Results that came from your actions. Discuss your accomplishments and how they were recognized by your peers. Remember to push your professional achievements, but never gloat.

## 5. <u>Where do you see yourself in five years?</u>

This is another question that you will want to be honest with. An employer is well aware of the fact that the position you are applying for may not be your dream job. Be honest because the hiring manager asks this question to see if you are a realistic person. They want to see if you are ambitious and if those expectations of yourself line up with the requirements for the job position.

It is acceptable if you don't know where you see yourself in five years. Rather than saying that you have no clue where you want to be to the hiring manager, focus on the job position. It is suggested that you state that you are hoping the position will help you make a decision with your future goals. By doing this, hiring managers may see that you care about the company and creating a future that includes the business.

If you are aware of where you see yourself in five years, be sure that your answer is relevant to the job. The last thing an interviewer wants to hear is that you are using the job to better yourself. The manager will want to know that you are working to help benefit the company. Mention the skills that are in line with the job position to help promote the vision of where you see yourself in five years with the company. It's important to not talk about yourself, but yourself as part of the business.

## 6. <u>What is your Dream Job?</u>

First suggestion: If your dream job does not relate to the current job position you are being interviewed for, do not mention it. This question is asked for a few different reasons. First, the hiring manager is curious as to what is motivating you to apply for the current job and if it is related to your dream job.

Second, the interviewer is looking to see if you have the skills to be successful in the job position you are applying for.

Your dream job should reference some of the elements the job position requires. For example, if the job you are applying for requires a customer service, you can simply state that your dream job would require high levels of interactions with customers. Your dream job does not have to be specific. Rather than stating a specific job title, discuss the different responsibilities you hope to hold in the future.

The best way to get your point across is by focusing on the present and the future. Share examples of the activities you do currently that you enjoy most. If possible, be sure that these are skills you will need for the job. Second, bring up a future with the company. Mention that you have a long term interest in a high level position. By bringing up the future, you are telling the hiring manager that you plan on being an investment for the company rather than just using the position to better yourself for someone else.

## 7. How do you face challenges at work?

Use this question to your benefit. A hiring manager knows that work is not always a smooth path. You will want to use past experiences to support how you handled challenges at work. It is suggested to use the STAR method again to answer this question, as it is a similar question to what professional achievements you have. In case you forgot or don't feel like scrolling up to read, STAR stands for Situation, Task, Action, and Result. Follow the steps to provide the best answer.

Once you follow the steps, you will want to focus on how you handled the situation in both a productive and professional manner. An employer will want to see that you are able to keep calm in challenging situations. If you were the leader during the situation at hand, be sure to state that. It is impressive to be the person to guide a group of employees through a stressful situation. This is certainly an aspect the hiring manager will be looking for their own company.

When answering this question, be sure to close with a happy ending. Choose a story where there was either a resolution or compromise. Be sure to make yourself the hero of the challenge without coming across as arrogant. Be proud, but not prideful.

## 8. <u>What do you enjoy doing outside of work?</u>

Sometimes, hiring managers will throw in personal questions. This is not to trick you or throw you off guard; it is simply to get to know you better. Interviewers will ask about your hobbies in order to see if you will fit in with the culture of the business and to see if you are willing to open up and display your personality.

It is important to realize that it is okay to open up and share some of your personal life with the hiring manager. Remember: there is such thing as sharing too much. For example, it is one thing to tell the interviewer that you enjoy wine tasting, and another to tell them you get smashed on the weekends. Share your hobbies but keep it professional. Use the question as an opportunity to show that you are a well-rounded individual.

Some activities that you do share should show that you are intelligent, cultured, and interesting. While wanting to show yourself off, also be aware of what some of the other people in the company are interested in doing. If you did research beforehand about your interviewer, perhaps try to relate to them. If you have an activity in common with that person, be sure to bring it up. When people are similar, they are more willing to bond. This will be a sure way to make you stand out in a crowd!

# Interview Questions Involving the Work Place

When it comes down to an interview, most people are only concerned with talking about themselves. You have a short amount of time to convince the hiring manager that you are the perfect candidate for the job. Sure, you can list off the amazing qualities you have but in order to be more impressive, you need to show the interviewer that you are not just about yourself. By doing your research on the company and knowing facts when asked about the work place, it will come across as caring about the company as a whole.

Below is a list of questions you should review when preparing for an interview. Use them as a frame of reference as it can never be predicted what questions will be asked. The important factor in this segment of questions is that you know of the company, what they stand for, and the type of employee they are looking for.

## 1. What do you know about the company?

This is not a trick question. A hiring manager will ask this question, not to see if you know about the company, but if you care about the company. It would be simple enough to read the company's about page online and regurgitate the information, but this is not what the interviewer is looking for. While doing your research, look for the company's goals and be sure to make your answer more personable. Look for key words from the website while forming your answer.

You'll want to show that you are not just another candidate for the job. Be aware of what is going on in the company, perhaps bring up how you are impressed with clients they work with, or organizations they support. By knowing the deeper details than what is in the about section, you will seem more valuable to the company if you care for it.

## 2. How did you hear about the position?

When answering this question, realize that this is not asked only for your benefit. It is important to remember during an interview that you are not the only person in the room. A hiring manager will normally ask this question to test your culture skills. Was the position in the paper? This will show that you probably read the news and are up to date on current events. If you heard the position from a friend in the company, make sure you name drop! An interviewing manager will be more likely to form a bond if there are previous connections made with the company.

When answering this question, you will want to show off your passion for the company. The best way to give an impressive answer to the question is by showing that you paid attention to the details of the job description. You will want to list what caught your eye about the role and why you felt you would be a good fit. By praising the hiring manager on their work, it will make the question more about them than you if they were the one in charge of writing up the job description.

## 3. Why do you want this job?

Be honest when answering this question. You are most likely sitting in a room across from a hiring manager for a reason other than just needing a job. If that were the case, you probably wouldn't be preparing for the interview so thoroughly. What companies are looking for is passionate people for the job position. Answer carefully to show that you are the right candidate.

During your answer, you will want to mention the key factors about why the job is a great fit for you. Be sure to know the skills required for the job position beforehand. This way, you will be able to align your experience and the skill with the role in particular. If you have stronger skills than experience, make sure you focus on those. You will want to pinpoint the main part of the job role and use examples of your skills that would enhance the job.

Remember to be enthusiastic about the company. As stated before, hiring managers are going to look for the most passionate people for the job. Make yourself stand out with your passion, knowledge and skills; this will make you more memorable out of a group of interviewees.

Last, you will want to connect your passion to a career trajectory. In your answer, you will want to show a hiring manager that this isn't just another job for you. Show your interviewer that you are in for the long haul. Remember, you are an investment for the company. State your greatest skills to show that you would be a great asset to the business.

## 4. <u>Why are you leaving your current job/ Why were you fired?</u>

This question will change depending on the person. Whether you were fired or just decided to take on new opportunities, you will want to keep your answer simple and positive. Your best bet is to be honest and keep the answer about yourself rather than your past employer.

The greatest mistake a person can make is to trash talk their past employers. This shows bad character and places you in a very negative light. Instead of saying that you left your last job because your boss was a jerk, simply change the topic away from anyone else but yourself. It is key that you discuss that you are eager to take on new opportunities. You will want to show that you are always willing to take chances and grow as an individual. Discuss how you feel the position as hand is a better fit for you because of reasons a, b, and c.

If you were fired, you need to be honest with the hiring manager. However, just because you were fired doesn't mean that it needs to be a deal breaker for the current job. Show the interviewer that you learned from the situation. You can easily say that being fired was a learning situation that you decided to use to your advantage for the next job. You should always end each answer you give during an interview on a positive note.

## 5. <u>When was a time you exercised leadership?</u>

Leadership is another key quality hiring managers will be looking for in future employees. This question will be asked to see if you will be able to direct others through a hardship. Use this question to your benefit to showcase your management skills.

The key to answering this question is to show your confidence. Do this by preparing the right story. Your choice should highlight the skills that are also related to the current job position. When you are finishing the story, be sure to end it strong. There is nothing that ruins an answer more then by stuttering at the finish of an exciting story about leadership. It is suggested that when you finish the story, connect it back to the company and position you are being interviewed for.

Be prepared for questions such as this to be worded in a negative way. You will want to think logically about any question you are given. The hiring manager is looking to see how you can handle conflict and failure. Remember to twist the answer in a positive manner, this will show that you can stay cool in a stressful situation.

## 6. What type of work environment are you looking for?

There are a few ways you can prepare yourself for this question. First, you will want to research the company. Check out their website to see what type of person they usually hire. Use the information to benefit yourself for your upcoming interview. While on their website, see if any social media such as: Facebook, Instagram, or Twitter is connected. Here, you can see the type of tone they use.

If you want to go for a more personal approach, you always have the option to show up to an interview early and observe the employees. Be aware of how they dress, act, and interact with other people. By doing this, you will be able to mimic their movements and see for yourself if it is an environment you could work in.

It is also suggested to speak with clients of the business. These people can range from suppliers to company partners. During your answer, you will want to identify with an environment similar to the company you are applying for. A hiring manager is looking to see if you would fit in with other employees so that you would be a happy, productive worker.

## 7. Why should we hire you?

Now is the time to really sell yourself to the hiring manager. The key factor to remember is that every hire is a risk for the company. Your name will be connected to the interviewer who hired you if you were ever to be fired. Make sure that the hiring manager will feel secure that you are indeed the best option for the job. The best answer can be given through three main points.

First, be able to deliver great results. Do this by stating your accomplishments and success stories. Keep the stories short and to the point by choosing ones that promote the skills needed in the current job position. Next, you will want to prove that you would fit in with co-workers. The hiring manager wants to know that you will be a team player who is willing to compromise, share ideas, and help others out during a time of need. Last, really drill in the fact that you are the best candidate for the job. If you have any unique skills, now would be the time to state it. If you have expert programing skills, mention it. Can you speak three languages? Show it off. Now is the time to prove you are the best investment for the company.

## 8. <u>What are your salary requirements?</u>

This is a golden question. The hiring manager is looking to see if you believe your skills are valuable. Of course, you are going to believe you should be paid top dollar, but be realistic when it comes to a new job.

First, you will want to do research on the job position. You can use sites such as Glassdoor and Payscale to see what other people in the same position are being paid. You will need to be honest with yourself about your worth. The factors you need to take into account include your education, experience, and skills.

When deciding on a salary, it is a safe bet you place yourself in the center. By giving a middle number, a hiring manager may accept it immediately. If not, be willing to negotiate but never feel you need to sell yourself for less than your self-decided worth. If you feel you are more skilled, be able to walk away if the company is not willing to pay for your assets.

# Tips for Controlling Nerves

Some people are better at interviews than others. There are interview veterans out there that still get nervous no matter what number interview they are on. Now that you've gone through and prepared yourself for the questions that you will be asked, here are some tips and tricks to keep your nerves calm during the big day.

First, make sure you have a bag packed with everything you will need during the interview. These are items that you don't necessarily need but will be helpful in being prepared for anything that comes your way. Some of these items include: a bottle of water, directions to the interview, examples of your work for further evidence of your success, extra money, photo ID, your cellphone, and it doesn't hurt to have a pen and notepad on hand. By being extra prepared, you will have less to worry about!

Before a big interview, it is suggested that you exercise before. The activity will help burn off negative energy, promotes good physical fitness, and releases endorphins. Walking into an interview with a good attitude is crucial. By walking in positive and happy, it can cause an instant connection with the hiring manager. Often times when people are nervous, they will come across unfriendly and inattentive. Do not let your nerves get the best of you.

During the interview, be sure to have a set of notes with you. By writing down cues, you will show that you thoroughly prepared for the interview. Be sure to not completely rely on the cards in front of you. Friendly contact is a necessity while speaking with a hiring manager. Be sure to take deep breaths before answering and be aware if you are speaking too quickly. If there is a difficult question, it is okay to give yourself a second to pause before answering. If you were unsure of what the question means, do not be afraid to ask for clarification.

After the interview, be sure to remain happy and positive. Think of the whole interview as an experience and put the situation into perspective. Be sure to remind yourself that not getting the job is not the worst thing in the world. If anything, you have another interview under your belt and will be more prepared for the next one. More importantly, always be sure to follow up with the hiring manager a few days later. This will show your true devotion to the job, making you that much more memorable.

# **Build a professional online presence with LinkedIn**

LinkedIn is one of the biggest social networks on the internet. But unlike Facebook it is a business oriented social networking site.

It was created in 2003 and has up until now over 300 Million users in over 200 different countries.

And these 300 Million people are all professionals looking for business opportunities, ideas or potential employees.

You do not want to miss out on that!

Furthermore LinkedIn has become like an online business card. Even if your next employer is not on LinkedIn it is very likely that he will google your name.

And if you want to leave a great impression you want to make sure that a well set up LinkedIn profile of yours appears in the search results.

If your LinkedIn profile is nicely set up with a good and professional picture of yourself and an appealing description, it will not only make your potential next employer feel like he knows you better, but it will also show him that you are actively in the market looking for opportunities.

This will make you much more employable in your employers mind.

Controlling the google search results for your name is obviously not the only benefit of LinkedIn.

The website itself has huge potential for someone looking for a job because you are surrounded by a lot of highly educated and well paid people that you will want to come in contact with. If you want to be financially successful you have to surround yourself with financially successful people.

And its never been easier, you just have to become active.

So the best thing to do now (if you haven't already) is to set up a good looking LinkedIn profile and make sure it can be found under your name on google.

This will be enough to impress your potential next employers if they are google for your name.

If you want to take it a step further become active on the website and look actively for job opportunities.

# **<u>Conclusion</u>**

Now that you've reached the end of the book, it is important that you are aware of the final question you will be asked at the end of the interview: Do you have any questions? The answer should always be yes. Be prepared and be strategic about your answer. If needed, one should bring a list about any questions they do have. Be sure to clarify any questions you have about previous topics. Perhaps you could ask questions such as: How will my performance be evaluated? Are there opportunities for advancement? What are the next steps in the hiring process? You should never be afraid to ask too many questions. If anything, this will show the hiring manager that you are enthusiastic about the job.

The most important factor to remember is that in order to give your best answers during an interview question, you need to be prepared. Do so by knowing your skills thoroughly, recall any big experiences that practiced leadership, and do your research on the company. If you are able to nail every interview question, you are sure to be looked at as the best candidate for the job.

Hopefully this book has granted you access and knowledge to the most common interview questions. Be sure to review the topics above before any interview and best of luck to you in your future career endeavours!

I would be really grateful if you would leave a review, positive or negative, on Amazon. Your feedback will help me to continuously improve my work.

Thank You and best of luck!

www.ingramcontent.com/pod-product-compliance
Lightning Source LLC
Chambersburg PA
CBHW080645190526
45169CB00009B/3512